Now I Know

All About Seeds

Written by Susan Kuchalla
Illustrated by Jane McBee

Troll Associates

Library of Congress Cataloging in Publication Data

Kuchalla, Susan.
    All about seeds.

    (Now I know)
    Summary: Brief text and pictures present several
kinds of seeds and show how they grow into plants.
    1. Seeds—Juvenile literature.   2. Germination—
Juvenile literature. [1. Seeds. 2. Germination.
3. Plants] I. McBee, Jane, ill. II. Title.
QK661.K83   582'.0467   81-11480
ISBN 0-89375-658-X   AACR2
ISBN 0-89375-659-8 (pbk.)

10   9

What is a seed?

3

An acorn is a seed.

A pine cone is a seed.

A seed can be a pit or a nut or a bean.

Do you know what grows from a seed?

Plants grow from seeds. A flower is a plant.

A bush is a plant, and so is a tree.

Do you know how seeds are planted?
Sometimes they just fall to the ground.

Sometimes they are carried and planted by the wind.

Sometimes they are carried and planted by water.

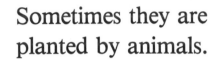

Sometimes they are
planted by animals.

And sometimes they are planted by people.

Seeds need water to grow. Rain gives them water.
Or people can bring water to them.

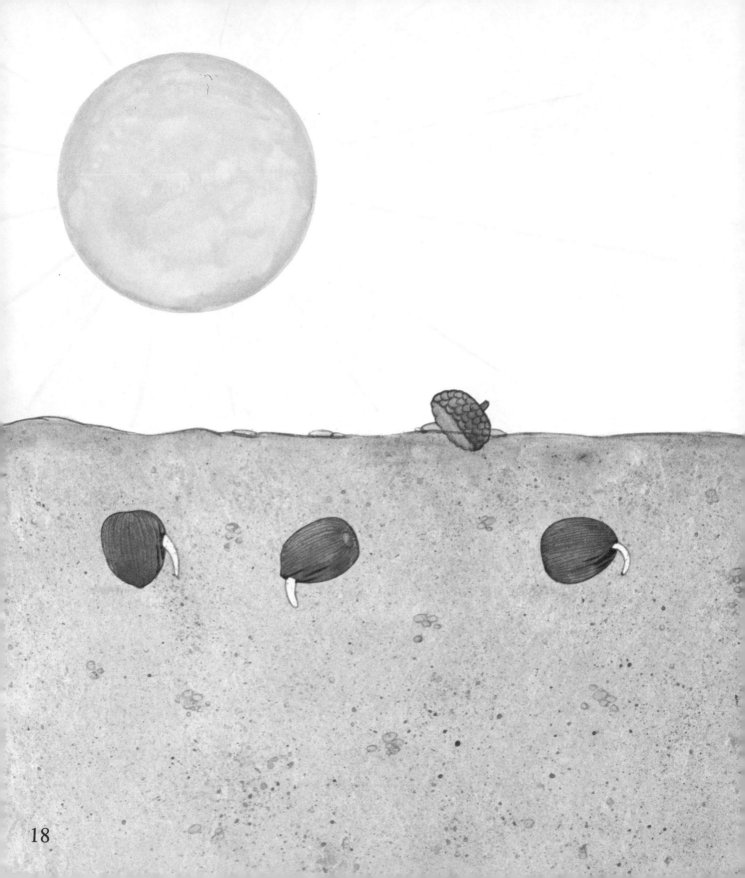

Seeds also need air and sunshine.
The sun warms the ground. The seed starts to grow.

There is a little plant in the seed.
It grows and grows.

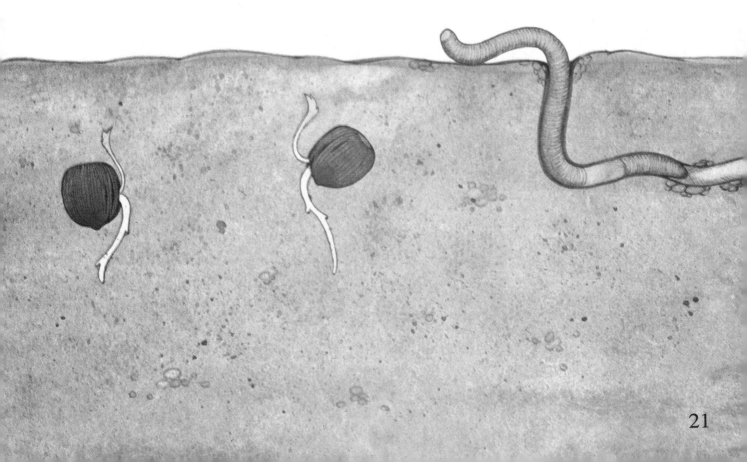

Soon the stem pushes up, and leaves grow.
Leaves reach out for sunlight. Plants make food from
water and sunlight.

The plant grows bigger and stronger.
What kind of plant will it be?

It might be a flower.

It might be a fruit or a vegetable.

It might be a pine tree.

It might be a tree that is covered with fruit.

But this plant grew from an acorn . . .

. . . so it will grow into a mighty oak tree!

Index